Farming Together

by Wanda Collins
Illustrated by Darryl Ligasan

Scott Foresman
is an imprint of

Glenview, Illinois • Boston, Massachusetts • Mesa, Arizona
Shoreview, Minnesota • Upper Saddle River, New Jersey

Illustrations
Darryl Ligasan

ISBN 13: 978-0-328-39372-5
ISBN 10: 0-328-39372-X

1 2 3 4 5 6 7 8 9 10 V010 17 16 15 14 13 12 11 10 09 08

Long ago, almost every family was a farming family. Families did not shop in stores. People had to grow enough food to last all year.

Today most people buy their food in stores. Many shoppers do not know that farming is hard work. Farming families work together to grow food for stores.

Anna's family is a farming family. They have an orange farm. Anna's family works together to take care of their orange trees.

Anna and her brothers go to school during the day. Their parents spend the whole day working too.

They must water the soil around the trees. They must also trim the trees.

Anna's father checks the weather every day. "The weather will be just right this week," he says.

Anna knows that the oranges need both sun and rain to grow.

Oranges need sun. **Oranges also need rain.**

What happens when the trees are full of oranges in October?

"It's harvest time!" says Anna's mother.

Harvest time is a very busy time. The family must work fast to pick the fruit.

Anna picks fruit that she can reach. Her big brothers pick fruit that is high above her head. There is so much work to do!

Farm workers start to feel tired toward the end of the harvest. But they must keep going until their work is done.

Anna's family sells their oranges to a store. Then they rest, but just for a little while. New oranges will start growing soon!

Anna does her schoolwork when the farm work is done. She is learning to spell. She can already spell this word...*orange!*